Les Cinq Doigts

for Piano

Chester Music

Les Cinq Doigts

8 Pièces très faciles sur 5 notes

Andantino

Igor Stravinsky

1.

Fine

Da capo al fine

CH02090

Allegro

Allegretto

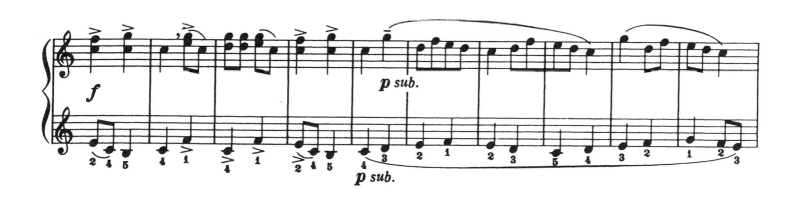

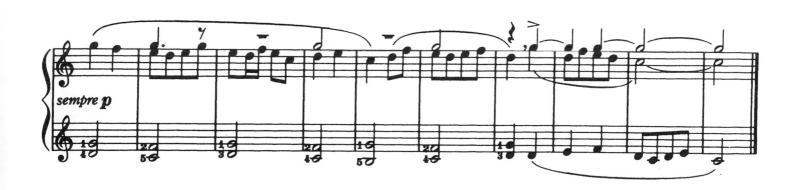

Larghetto

Moderato

5.

Fine

Del signo al fine

Lento

6.

Vivo

7.

Pesante

8.

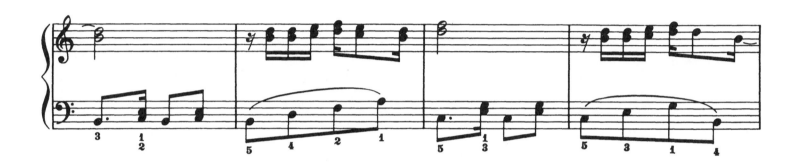

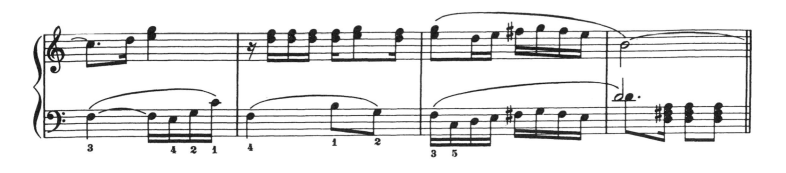

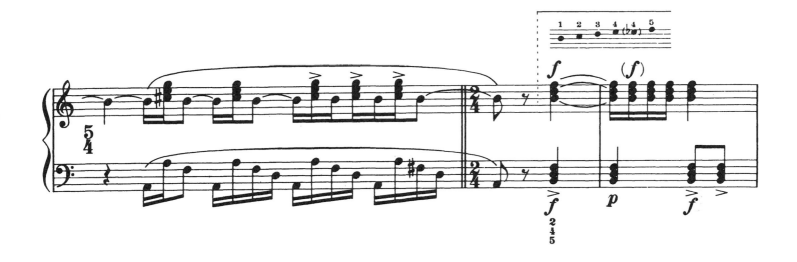